Disclaimer:

The following story is based on true events and real-life experiences. While every effort has been made to accurately represent the events and individuals involved, certain details may have been modified or fictionalized for the purpose of storytelling. The primary aim of this narrative is to convey the essence and essence of the actual events, and it should not be considered a wholly factual account. Names of individuals and specific locations may have been altered to protect their privacy and confidentiality. The content presented here is not intended to offend or harm anyone, and it is purely for entertainment and informational purposes. Readers are advised to exercise discretion and critical judgment while engaging with this story. The author and publisher disclaim any liability for the accuracy, completeness, or reliability of the information provided herein. Any resemblance to actual persons, living or dead, or to actual events is entirely coincidental.

Vittorio Emanuele

A King in Exile

Part III

Alexandra Sterling

Preface

In the annals of history, few figures have elicited as much fascination and ardor as Vittorio Emanuele III, the King of Italy whose life and reign were indelibly marked by the tumultuous events of his time. His tale of exile, recounted in this remarkable trilogy by the esteemed American scholar, Alexandra Sterling, is a captivating journey through the trials and tribulations faced by a monarch forced to navigate the treacherous waters of political upheaval.

As Alexandra Sterling delves into the depths of Vittorio Emanuele's exile, her compelling narrative weaves together the intricate threads of history with a keen eye for detail and an unyielding commitment to authenticity. With her unbridled curiosity and a passion for historical truth, she transports readers into the heart of Italy's tumultuous past, where the echoes of revolution and the whispers of power struggles resonate in the corridors of regal palaces.

Through meticulous research and a relentless pursuit of the truth, Alexandra Sterling presents a portrait of Vittorio Emanuele III that goes beyond the surface of historical accounts, delving into the complexities of a man caught in the maelstrom of political turmoil. Her eloquent prose breathes life into the past, offering readers an intimate glimpse into the private struggles and public challenges faced by the exiled monarch.

This novella, presented in three captivating installments, unveils the intricacies of Vittorio Emanuele III's exile, drawing readers deeper into the essence of a man grappling with the consequences of choices made in moments of unprecedented upheaval.

As the trilogy unfolds, Alexandra Sterling's literary craftsmanship shines brightly, illuminating the interconnectedness of global events and the human drama that unfolded during these critical years. Her portrayal of Vittorio Emanuele III's exile is both empathetic and enlightening, capturing the essence of a man struggling with the weight of history.

In this masterful work, Alexandra Sterling invites readers to embark on an unforgettable journey through history, to bear witness to the triumphs and tribulations of a king in exile, and to discover the timeless relevance of his story in the tapestry of human experience.

Chapter 13

FORWARD SAVOY!

Mario De Simoni, Angelo Binaschi, Renzo De Vecchi, Guido Ara, Giuseppe Milano I, Pietro Leone, Enrico Debernardi, Aldo Cevenini I, Felice Berardo, Carlo Rampini I, Carlo Corna. These were the eleven players of the Italian national football team who, for the first time, donned the azure jersey in honor of the royal house. The National Team was playing its third match in history: an exhibition match against Hungary at the Arena in Milan on January 6, 1911.

The azure color of the Blessed Virgin was chosen by Amedeo VI of Savoy (1334-1383) against the Turks and remains the color of Italy for the officers of the armed forces and the athletes of the national teams to this day. Amedeo VI was nicknamed the "Green Count" because of the color of his uniform during parades. In 1366, he went to the aid of his cousin, John V Palaiologos, the emperor of the East, who was threatened by the Turks. The Green Count wanted to have two flags on his flagship: the red one with the silver cross of the House of Savoy, and a second one entirely azure in honor of the Most Holy Annunciation (to whom he dedicated the chivalric order he founded in 1364). Since then, the Savoy officers have worn a knotted azure scarf around their waist or neck, later becoming mandatory by a decree issued in 1572 by Duke Emanuele Filiberto of Savoy (1528-1580), also known as Ironhead. The use of the azure scarf for officers became so deeply rooted that it persisted even during the transition from monarchy to republic. No other army in the world has such an ancient service badge as the Savoy azure scarf.

This is just one example: everyone knows who the "Azzurri" are (the nickname for the Italian national teams), but few know that the origin of that color as a national symbol comes from the

House of Savoy. I am the first to acknowledge that Italy is now a republic and no longer a monarchy, but that doesn't mean we should erase everything that was associated with the monarchy. Like the azure scarf, there are hundreds of traditions that stem from the Savoy family, a dynasty with a thousand-year history.

In the end, the history of European crowns is remarkable: some small dynasties that once ruled over limited regions or small cities grew so powerful that they ended up ruling half the world, until the French Revolution and Napoleon came along. Then, the two World Wars wiped away the past, and now, almost everywhere, there is a parliamentary democracy, with the monarchy - where it still exists - becoming a representative institution of the nation.

The Habsburgs originated from Switzerland, the Bourbons from France, the Saxe-Coburg-Gotha from two German towns, and the Savoys from the southeastern part of France, near the border with Italy. All were small feudal dynasties that, through military victories and, above all, strategic marriages, rose to international power.

If we trace back my genealogy, we encounter all the protagonists of European history, mainly because among the families of royal houses, we are all relatives, all cousins from first to fourth degree. I am also one of the very few who have reigning dynasties on both the paternal and maternal sides. Going from my father upwards (Umberto II, Vittorio Emanuele III, Umberto I, Vittorio Emanuele II, Carlo Alberto), all were kings from father to son. My mother's father (Alberto) was the King of Belgium, and her two brothers were kings (Leopold) and regent (Charles Theodore), while the sons of Leopold (first Baudouin, currently Albert) are also kings.

In the mid-19th century, the Saxe-Coburg-Gotha family, my grandfather's family from Belgium, was on the thrones of Belgium, England, Portugal, and Bulgaria. My grandmother's family, the Wittelsbach-Birkenfeld-Gelnhausen, were dukes of Bavaria who also intermarried with the royals of Bavaria. For example, Elizabeth (Sissi), the wife of Franz Joseph, the Austro-Hungarian emperor, was my maternal grandmother's aunt, and Maria Sofia, the wife of Francis II, the last king of the Two Sicilies.

As for the Savoys, if we go further back, we find a Berta who married Emperor Henry IV in 1066 (the one who went to Canossa to meet Pope Gregory VII) and Matilda. Adelaide, Berta's sister, married Rudolph of Swabia. The next generation sees Agnes marrying Aimone II of Bourbon, and Adelaide marrying Louis VI the Fat, King of France. Mafalda married King Alfonso I of Portugal in 1146. Giovanna, daughter of Amedeo V, married the Byzantine Emperor Andronikos III Paleologos in 1326, and they had a son named Giovanni, defended against the Turks by his cousin Amedeo VI, the one with the azure scarf. Giovanna, the granddaughter of Amedeo V, married Giovanni III of Brittany in 1329.

The daughters of Amedeo VIII (1383-1451), also known as the "Pacific," the founder of the Order of Saints Maurice and Lazarus and anti-pope for ten years as Felix V, were Maria, who married a Visconti, and Margherita, who married three times (Luigi III of Anjou, Ludovico IV of Wittelsbach, and Ulrich of Württemberg). Their granddaughters were Bona, who married Galeazzo Maria Sforza, and Margherita, who was married to Giovanni IV of Monferrato and then Pietro of Luxembourg. At the age of ten (in 1451), Margherita married the Dauphin of France, the future King Louis XI. In another generation, we have Anna, who married Frederick of Aragon, and Louise of Savoy, who married Charles of Orléans in 1488 and became the mother of King Francis I of France.

Margherita married Francesco Gonzaga, Duke of Mantua, in 1608, Isabella married Alfonso d'Este, Duke of Modena, and Maria Adelaide married Louis of Burgundy in 1685. Her sister Maria Luisa Gabriella married Philip V, the King of Spain, who was the nephew of Louis XIV and the founder of the Bourbon branch of Spain. The three sons of Vittorio Amedeo III of Savoy married the two brothers and a sister of King Louis XVI of France (the one who was guillotined in 1793): Giuseppina married Louis XVIII in 1771, Maria Teresa married Charles X in 1773, and Charles Emmanuel IV married Maria Clotilde of Bourbon. The last marriages of the Savoy branch that died out were those of Beatrice, who married Francesco IV of Modena in 1812, Maria Teresa, who married Carlo II of Parma, Marianna, who married Emperor Ferdinand of Austria of the Habsburg family, and Maria Cristina, who married Ferdinand II of

Bourbon, the King of the Two Sicilies. At this point, the Savoy Carignano branch remains, with Carlo Alberto as the progenitor, becoming the kings of Sardinia and, from March 17, 1861, the kings of Italy.

It seems like a long list of characters, now distant in history. However, it is only a small part of the thousands of names that have been connected through marriage in centuries of European history. It serves to understand that all royal houses are related to each other. If we consider the four quarters of my birth, that is, the four families of my grandparents, we will realize that for centuries, we were already related to all the other royal houses. There is an abyss between the marriage politics of European crowns until the 19th century and the military, colonial, and diplomatic politics of the 20th century.

The first advantage of such a widespread family relationship was the possibility of being updated on everything and everyone. Ceremonies were quite frequent - coronations, baptisms, engagements, weddings, and funerals - so at least once a year, the royal families would meet, talk, dialogue, make proposals, weave alliances, and conspire.

In essence, the style imposed on royal families remained similar for centuries. I myself was raised as they were in the old days. Thus, as befits an heir apparent, I didn't receive direct education from my father and mother. It started with nurses, then governesses, and then tutors. When I grew up and had a son to educate, I did exactly what others in the family hadn't done. I took care of my son's education and development personally. I gave him the opportunities to do everything that I would have wanted - and mostly couldn't - do both in terms of education and leisure activities. I personally taught him how to ski, swim, and fly planes, and so on. I gave my son Emanuele Filiberto all the love and affection that I had missed in my life and more. I looked back at my youth and ensured my son had the opposite experience.

I never said "no" to my father Umberto IV because I never had the opportunity to do so. He made decisions without asking for my opinion, just as it had happened to Umberto II with Vittorio Emanuele III. My father obeyed and didn't argue. It's quite impressive - and I imagine how much he suffered - to see the photographs of Hitler's visit to Rome in May 1938. Among the two bigwigs (and much more, as history showed) like Mussolini and Hitler, accompanied by sycophants like von Ribbentrop, the crown prince stood in the second row. Umberto was clearly uncomfortable, as was my grandfather, the king. It's not just discomfort in etiquette, not merely a formality, but also a profound feeling. When my grandfather embarrassed Hitler by asking how many nails were in the boots of German soldiers and then explained how many and where there were in the Italian boots, it was his way of showing Mussolini and Hitler that the king-soldiers understood war down to the last detail.

When my grandfather and grandmother went into exile in Egypt, leaving only their son Umberto as king, he found himself overwhelmed by a mountain of problems that he was not aware of, nor did he know the political positions of his father on each one of them. My grandfather did not pass the reins of abdication on May 9, 1946. The famous phrase was: "Now, you have fun."

Despite the end of the monarchy and both of us being adults, my father never managed to talk freely about Italian history and our family. Today, the reality is different; I talk with my son Emanuele Filiberto every day, and he does not hesitate to contradict me if he deems it necessary, explaining his reasons.

The only information I received from my family is mainly from the stories my mother, Maria José, told me, but even then, not overly so. For instance, she talked about the bombings in Naples, during which she worked tirelessly to assist the injured, with great difficulty. She rarely talked about politics, but she did explain Benedetto Croce's hypothesis of the double abdication of my grandfather, Vittorio Emanuele III, in favor of my father, Umberto II, and then my father's abdication in favor of me, with my mother Maria José being the regent until I reached adulthood.

My mother was anti-fascist, but their attempts to engage with intellectuals and political forces to liberate Italy from the fascist regime and the alliance with Hitler were always thwarted. Looking back, valid alternatives to the decisions made by the royal family could have been found. For example, in a book titled "Sull'onore dei Savoia," the author, Arturo Catalano Gonzaga di Cirella, a midshipman aboard the battleship Roma, explains that the Italian Navy fleet during the war was still complete, having lost only a few ships.

In conclusion, I was the first in the Savoy family not to have a military tutor, although both Piccard and Montezemolo had fought valiantly in World War II. Nevertheless, my military upbringing instilled discipline, and my

character lacks neither tenacity nor courage. I don't back down from anything when I'm convinced of something; I pursue it to the end, whatever the cost. My father, Umberto, on the other hand, had a strong military spirit, but he was also a highly educated person who could not even think of resorting to violence. He was very honest in his dealings with representatives of power, be it Italian, German, or Allied forces, and he would never break a promise. Etiquette, protocol, and diplomacy were strong rules for him; he would never behave poorly or act excessively. He would never make a decision against the wishes of his parents, nor would he want to cause discord within the Savoy family. His absolute and unquestionable obedience to his father, who was also the king, was an inviolable limit.

In essence, our parents were unable to raise their children because they did not know how to do it. They had always been raised to prepare for the crown, the throne, and this education required a certain number of people to take care of the children until they reached adulthood. I will always remember the time my mother, Maria José, told me in Merlinge, "You know, I love you very much, but I can't express it; I have great affection for you, but I can't show it." It was not that she meant to say, "We, the Coburg-Saxony family, are tough," but in a sense, it was just that because she had received a strict upbringing from her father, King Albert I of Belgium. That's how they were; they had been educated as royals and princes. In contrast, we were evicted from the palaces and had to work like everyone else. Fortunately, we knew how to choose the right path to move forward.

The education of Savoy males, by tradition, has always been military, with a military preceptor, of course, a career officer, who would stay with the heir apparent until they were twenty-one. At fifteen, Umberto I of Savoy, just having turned, took part in the Second War of Independence against the Austrians, as an officer of the Third Piedmont Infantry Regiment. The war, which concluded in 1859, featured one of the bloodiest battles in military history, the Battle of Solferino and San Martino. Almost two hundred thousand soldiers faced off, and after fourteen hours of fighting, losses totaled over thirty thousand men. From Carlo Alberto onwards, all the Savoys, especially the heirs to the throne, were educated in warfare and engaged in it. My father suffered because he wanted to fight in the resistance, but they did not allow it, claiming that the heir apparent, the only male, could not and should not die to avoid the extinction of the dynastic succession.

As for me, Vittorio Emanuele IV, I can say - once again - that I never said "no" to my father because I never had the opportunity to do so. He decided without asking for my opinion, just as it happened with Umberto II and Vittorio Emanuele III. My father obeyed and did not argue. It is quite impressive to see the photographs of Hitler's visit to Rome in May 1938. Among the two bigwigs (and much more, as history showed) like Mussolini and Hitler, accompanied by sycophants like von Ribbentrop, the crown prince stood in the second row. Umberto was clearly uncomfortable, as was my grandfather, the king. It's not just discomfort in etiquette, not merely a formality, but also a profound feeling. When my grandfather embarrassed Hitler by asking how many nails were in the boots of German soldiers and then explained how many and where there were in the Italian boots, it was his way of showing Mussolini and Hitler that the king-soldiers understood war down to the last detail.

When my grandfather and grandmother went into exile in Egypt, leaving only their son Umberto as king, he found himself overwhelmed by a mountain of problems that he was not aware of, nor did he know the political positions of his father on each one of them. My grandfather did not pass the reins of abdication on May 9, 1946. The famous phrase was: "Now, you have fun."

Despite the end of the monarchy and both of us being adults, my father never managed to talk freely about Italian history and our family. Today, the reality is different; I talk with my son

Emanuele Filiberto every day, and he does not hesitate to contradict me if he deems it necessary, explaining his reasons.

The only information I received from my family is mainly from the stories my mother, Maria José, told me, but even then, not overly so. For instance, she talked about the bombings in Naples, during which she worked tirelessly to assist the injured, with great difficulty. She rarely talked about politics, but she did explain Benedetto Croce's hypothesis of the double abdication of my grandfather, Vittorio Emanuele III, in favor of my father, Umberto II, and then my father's abdication in favor of me, with my mother Maria José being the regent until I reached adulthood.

My mother was anti-fascist, but their attempts to engage with intellectuals and political forces to liberate Italy from the fascist regime and the alliance with Hitler were always thwarted. Looking back, valid alternatives to the decisions made by the royal family could have been found. For example, in a book titled "Sull'onore dei Savoia," the author, Arturo Catalano Gonzaga di Cirella, a midshipman aboard the battleship Roma, explains that the Italian Navy fleet during the war was still complete, having lost only a few ships.

And he tells that the fleet was heading to La Maddalena, which had been occupied by a contingent of German troops just a few hours before: a fleet of that size could have defeated those few invaders with just a few shots. If my grandfather, Vittorio Emanuele III, had gone to La Maddalena instead of Brindisi, he would have changed history, as the entire fleet and a large part of the military aviation remained loyal to the king. From Sardinia, well defended by the Navy and Air Force, my grandfather could have commanded and governed differently than from Apulia, which was already under the Allies' control. Instead, the fleet en route to La Maddalena was forced to turn back without specifying where it would go, out of fear of those Germans stationed on the island who were not invincible, in fact! And so, they lost the battleship Roma. At that time, there was Supermarina, which couldn't keep information secret. I believe that Supermarina was directly connected with the British. But if we look at everything that the wonderful Italian sailors did - and they did it very well - in Sardinia, our fleet would have been a strong point to negotiate with the Allies from a more authoritative Italian perspective. All of this, the double abdication and isolation in Sardinia, should have happened, of course, before the summer of 1943 when the Anglo-American Allies landed in Sicily.

Of course, these hypotheses we make in retrospect, but then we should also consider the people, the characters, the psychologies, and the moments of that reality in that historical context. To be more explicit: let's remember that at the mere mention of abdication, there was always a little devil of the Aosta family looming and saying, "abdicate so that we can take the throne." I am sure, based on what I knew of my father Umberto, that he would have renounced the throne in this hypothesis of double abdication if he were convinced it was for the good of Italy. He wasn't attached to the throne - mind you, the throne was not in question as it rightfully belonged to him by dynastic right being the heir apparent, the only male child of Vittorio Emanuele III. My father was awarded the Gold Medal for valor in the battle of Montelungo at Monte Cassino, where he fought alongside a Polish regiment. The Gold Medal, conferred on him by the Poles, I donated to the Museum of the Battle of Monte Cassino, in the section dedicated to the fallen Polish soldiers. My father wasn't afraid of anything; that's for sure.

Now, let's talk about the figure of the tutors, which the Savoy tradition wanted by the side of the young heir prince until his adulthood. Vittorio Emanuele II, whose manners were not as refined, was surrounded in vain by a group of tutors and had General Giuseppe Rossi as his "governor." The tutor of Vittorio

Emanuele III was Colonel Egidio Osio, who was a military attaché in Berlin. Finally, my father had Admiral Attilio Bonaldi as his "governor."

My two tutors instilled in me a noble and dignified vision of life: responsibility, courage, audacity, and culture. They were very active individuals, never rigid, and taught me a lot about mechanics and science, but they also encouraged me to engage in various sports and learn how to ride motorcycles, drive cars, and fly airplanes.

Already, there is a difference with my ancestors. There was discipline for the sake of discipline: waking up at dawn, washing with cold water, preparing equipment, riding horses, hunting, using weapons. With Piccard, and later with Montezemolo, the discipline was no less tough, but it was always aimed at achieving a verifiable and immediate purpose. Spending almost a year in America with Piccard to understand what the sea is like involves sacrifices and risks, but I saw them preparing a bathyscaphe that reached the deepest point of the oceans. You learn everything, from sailor knots to cooking fish, to the laws of physics. But, as I repeat, not to become a parade soldier. They taught me things that would be useful in life.

At the Saint Moritz airport, there was visual landing, not the instrumental one. The pilot made a mistake due to poor visibility and hit the right wing on the frozen Lake Silvaplana. The plane bounced and broke into two pieces after being dragged for a kilometer. Luckily, a group of cross-country skiers, consisting of doctors from the hospital, provided first aid. My mother, Iris, suffered several fractures and couldn't be taken to a hospital for three months. Marina, who was five months pregnant, was terribly frightened. My mother suffered less severe injuries. That's how the birthday dinner turned into a hospital visit.

To lighten the mood a bit at that point, I had an idea for my father, who was taken by surprise. I asked Corrado Agusta, "Could you please help me? Can you lend me a helicopter to take my father on a ride with Frixa?" Frixa was the chief helicopter pilot at Agusta and someone my father trusted completely. "No problem," Corrado replied and, turning to the pilot, added, "Frixa, accompany His Majesty and the Prince on a helicopter ride."

I sat in the back seat, and at the beginning of the flight, we told Dad that we were going to see where the plane had crashed, a Mystère 20, carrying my mother and my mother-in-law, Iris. However, our helicopter, after flying over the crash site, continued in a different direction. My father understood that we were passing over Italy, even though we were in flight, but he didn't say anything. He was both emotional and fearful at the same time, but he remained silent and observant. I remember that flight very well; it was an exceptional event. Frixa was a great pilot and taught me everything about helicopters. He had been in the aviation war and spoke about it often before joining Agusta. I believe his son is also a pilot at Alitalia.

I only have an airplane pilot's license, whereas my son, Emanuele Filiberto, has both airplane and helicopter pilot licenses. When we returned from the long flight, my father was very happy: he had arrived in Saint Moritz worried but left for Portugal happy to have seen Italy as he had never seen it before, flying low in a helicopter. We flew at an altitude of about 150-200 meters, which is the right height from the ground to get a better view of the terrain. And Umberto could only catch a glimpse of Italy from the sea when he was on the French Riviera. It is significant that at the end of the flight, he didn't say a word; he only thanked the chief pilot, Frixa, for the nice ride. He didn't say anything to me: either he was very moved or didn't know what to say; he wasn't prepared to see what he had seen.

Like my mother, who also wrote books about the Savoy family, my father was very passionate about history. Unfortunately, there are no traces of this passion. In his will, there was mostly a precise and detailed list - hundreds of pages - of many family items

. He left everything to the Sicilian State just before the final departure into exile in June 1946, doubting the legitimate owner of the Savoy family jewels. Doubtful, indeed, he didn't even take his personal jewelry with him. He left with two suitcases and a few personal effects. Some other things were sent to him by friends who remained in Italy. My suspicion is that many of our belongings left in various residences due to the haste of departure have disappeared due to the actions of several people. I remember, for example, the year I left Rome for exile when I was playing with mechanical contraptions at the Quirinale, even simple ones, doing bricolage. In that period, I was curious about all the objects that came into my hands, and it was a great excitement when four or five blue crates arrived. Witnessing the opening with trepidation, but inside those containers, there were only towels and newspaper clippings. My strong suspicion is that everything had already been stolen. My father left with three outfits and a few personal effects. How could he have taken along the boxes - and many of them would have been needed - of the famous archives, more or less secret?

I too would like to know the truth about the documents of our house, but for now, I adhere to my father's certain and certified wishes: to safeguard the few traditions that survived the transition from monarchy to republic.

There has never been this great fortune of the Savoia family, and a lot of money was spent on my father's exile, which lasted for thirty-seven years, and on the many donations he was asked for and couldn't refuse. Umberto's will doesn't concern alleged fortunes – the inheritance we children received in money was modest – but instead, it lists in three volumes all the objects of the House of Savoia, to whose cataloging my father had dedicated himself during the long exile. Then there are provisions concerning the Collars of the Annunziata and the chivalric orders.

Regarding my mother's succession, I prefer not to talk about it; it is still an open question. I fear that during her stay in Mexico since 1992, where she was convinced to move by my sister Maria Beatrice and her husband, Luf Reyna, many things were taken away from her, including the objects from the house in Merlinge.

While Maria José was in Mexico, I had bought Merlinge and rented it out because, by then, it was desolately empty. My sister Titti's husband had taken all the furnishings from Geneva to Mexico. And that's not all; he had my mother buy some sort of shack, making her pay a lot of money for it, and then he only put two or three things inside, leaving her there. Mexico has stolen many years of Maria José's life and dissolved the beautiful things in Merlinge, the memories, and the family heirlooms. Everything disappeared.

With my sister Ella, then, we took advantage of one of the times when my mother was coming to Belgium and picked her up at Brussels airport. We took her to a hotel, took her passport away, and told her to come and stay with me in Geneva. This happened in 1996. We rescued her from those who were taking advantage of her, and fortunately, she never went back to Mexico, where terrible things happened. Mr. Reyna, involved in various trafficking activities and shady people, was beaten to death, and it was never clear why or by whom. Perhaps it's better not to know. Maria José was very happy to return to living in Geneva; she stayed with me and also with Maria Gabriella. Ella is the sister I get along with best: we are similar! Unfortunately, even in appearance, we have the same face. In all families, there are misunderstandings, but we are the closest among the four siblings. And we are the only two living in Geneva; we did our university studies together, skied together, and went on magnificent cruises together, even with her ex-husband de Balkany, and with Marina, in the Caribbean.

Pertini, as President of the Republic, had promised my mother everything under the sun, but then nothing happened. The worst thing he did was make fun of my father, Umberto: he told him he could return to Italy before his supposedly imminent death. My father had brought back his old gray suit from Portugal in anticipation of his return. Then, once again, nothing happened, and they didn't even let him see beloved Italy one last time, as a human gesture toward a dying man. Such a shame!

I went to the European Parliament, obtaining recognition of my rights, and later to the European Court of Human Rights, and my request was accepted there too. Moreover, the foundational treaty of Europe (Treaty of Rome, 1957) is based on one principle, a single but fundamental principle: that of the free movement of people and goods in Europe. Don't we, the Savoia family, have the right to it?

Emanuele Filiberto was born in exile on June 22, 1972, in Geneva. First of all, we had not disclosed the news of the pregnancy, and we didn't know if it would be a boy or a girl. My wife Marina went to the maternity hospital in Geneva, and I had attended a course at the university to prepare for the birth. I believe it's something everyone should do; it's only right for the husband to assist his wife during childbirth. When our son was born, my mother was with us, and I called my father. "Ah, good, good, then it's a son," those were his words. He concluded with "Very well, bravo." I named him Emanuele Filiberto, a name often repeated among my ancestors.

Umberto came to the baptism and became the godfather of my son, giving him the title of Prince of Venice. My mother also attended and was the godmother. The ceremony took place in Merlinge, in great harmony and serenity. Naturally, many people attended the baptism in Merlinge; there were many people at the ceremony. Even earlier, at the wedding celebration that Marina and I had in Geneva after our civil wedding in Las Vegas and religious wedding in Tehran, Maria José, King Simeone of Bulgaria (my first cousin and the son of my aunt Giovanna), and Aunt Malia of Bourbon Parma (my father's sister) all came.

For the first time, a Savoia male (and firstborn) did not have a tutor. Emanuele Filiberto has always been close to his parents, even when traveling. For example, when I was in Saint Moritz for work with the Shah and Corrado Agusta, my son was two and a half years old, and I slowly taught him to ski.

When he was older, we enrolled him in the International School of Geneva. He did well until the first kidnapping attempt. With the addition of bodyguards, he continued for another year at the international school, but then we decided it would be safer to transfer him to Rosey, where his father had studied. There was always an open dialogue with us as parents, and we agreed that if he ever felt uncomfortable at the boarding school, he could call us, we would talk about it, and I would potentially take him away. However, Emanuele stayed at Rosey until the end, but he asked to attend private courses in Lausanne for his final year in preparation for his matriculation exams, as he would not have otherwise passed them. He successfully passed his scientific high school exams, just as I had done. Then came the second kidnapping attempt.

Emanuele Filiberto is the first Savoy to be born and raised in exile. He received the education we thought was appropriate, starting with his upbringing as a human being. I have always spoken to him in Italian since his birth. He studied history and was always very aware of his position within the House of Savoy. I took him to various events and ceremonies.

Simeone was born on June 16, 1937 - we are the same age - in Sofia. He studied in Alexandria, Egypt, where his mother had gone with my grandfather (both in exile!). Let us remember that Simeone's father, King Boris III of Bulgaria, was likely assassinated by Hitler using poisoned oxygen on the airplane returning from Germany to Sofia after a tumultuous meeting between the two leaders. King Boris died on August 28, 1943, when Simeone was six years old. Then, in September 1944, there was the communist coup: all his relatives, the regents, were killed by the new regime. On September 16, 1946, a referendum, three months after the one in Italy, under the threat of the Red Army, chose the republican form of government, just like in Italy. They were then transferred to Egypt and later in 1951 to Madrid, where they were granted asylum. Simeone later studied at an American military academy in Pennsylvania. He once said a profound statement: "Exile is the best formation for a king, provided that he can return to his homeland!"

My grandmother Elena, in addition to loving fishing, enjoyed driving a Balilla with three gears and doing slaloms in the pine forest. In her diary, she also wrote, when she was in Naples waiting to leave Italy forever, that what mattered to her was not monarchy or republic, but only that the Italians were happy. Puzzles, like all things to assemble, including guns, were one of her great passions. In her Montenegro, it was normal for members of the royal family, even the females, to carry weapons on their belts. Once in San Rossore, they showed a new pistol to my grandfather Vittorio Emanuele III, a Luger, and partially disassembled it. Neither my grandfather, a soldier king, nor the officer could put it back together. My grandmother Elena succeeded in reassembling it.

Prince Nikola I of Montenegro (Njegos 1841-Cap d'Antibe 1921), Elena's father, died in the Blue Coast and was buried in San Remo. He was sent into exile in 1918 when his land became part of the Kingdom of Serbia, Croatia, and Slovenia. However, with great tenacity, his small country had defeated the Turks and gained independence. For this reason, high-ranking Yugoslav officials of Montenegrin origin brought his remains back to Montenegro in 1989, to Cetinje, considering him a national hero. Nicola Petrovic Njegos had ruled for fifty-eight years, from 1860 to 1918, first as a prince, and in 1910, he proclaimed himself the first (and last) king of Montenegro.

I remember that Marina and I went to Montenegro for the return of Nikola I's remains from San Remo. The body arrived by plane, a DC9, to Bari, and from there, it was transported on an Italian military ship, the San Marco, with military honors, to Bar (in Italian, Antivari), on the coast. Around 150,000 people, all of them communists, were there to receive the former king's remains, but for them, it was not a problem that he had been a king because winning against the Turks meant more than anything else.

My mother Maria José knew Marina from when she was little because their families were neighbors, and they often saw each other. My grandmother Elisabeth of Belgium, seeing me often in Brussels for work, took the opportunity to invite Marina for an extended visit, for a month! They got along very well, drove together in the car, and talked about everything. My father, on the other hand, got to know her well on the occasion of Emanuele Filiberto's baptism. That event changed everything and improved their relationship. Umberto talked for hours with her and even gifted her a portion of Queen Margherita's necklace and some other family jewelry, just as he had done for my mother.

The usual courtiers had objected that Marina was not noble, and I couldn't marry her. So I conducted thorough research and prepared a dossier, stating that the Marquises Ricolfi Doria were an ancient family from Genoa, and so on. But that dossier disappeared, and my father never received it. I remember that Honorable Lauro, a monarchist, was sent to Geneva to convince me not to marry. First, they cut off my funds, and then they even turned against my future wife.

By that time, I was already living with Marina, and after the wedding, we moved to the house we still have today, in Vésenaz, on the shores of Lake Geneva, near Merlinge. My mother, who saw Marina frequently, gladly visited us to see her grandchild.

During the fifteen years I worked with Corrado Agusta, Marina was always with me, participating in various activities. Marina also serves as my liaison officer with Italy; she visits the country often, meets various people on my behalf, engages in charitable activities, and follows the developments of the Order of Saints Maurice and Lazarus.

The daughter of a Swiss industrialist and banker, Marina is descended from the Marquises Doria of Genoa and was a world champion in water skiing. Marina's grandfather fought in the wars of the Italian Risorgimento with the Savoia Cavalry, and we still preserve his helmet, sabers, and medals from four battles.

On one of my trips to America with Agusta, Marina, whom Corrado cared for, accompanied us. We had been engaged for thirteen years by then. We were going to test fly the Agusta AB112 helicopter, a twin-engine, in Las Vegas. At one point, I jokingly said to Marina, "Since we're here, why don't we get married? Check the procedures." That evening, Marina replied, "That's all they do here." So everything was organized. With Corrado Agusta and his secretary Franco Chiesa, we bought two wedding rings in one store and a pre-packaged bouquet in another. Then we went before a justice of the peace, who married us. It was January 11, 1970, in Las Vegas, Nevada, a civil wedding that I didn't inform anyone about, not even my parents. Marina's parents, on the other hand, knew about it from us. Later, we also had a religious ceremony in Tehran, on October 7, 1971, at the Chapel of Don Bosco Institute. Why Tehran? Firstly, because I was working for Agusta there, and there was significant work to be done, requiring my constant presence. Secondly, having found an exceptional person, almost a friend, in Shah Reza Pahlavi, I took advantage of the invitation to the Iranian national festivities at Persepolis, where all the European aristocrats were invited, to marry two days before the festivities began. This was accomplished: if everyone said that by marrying Marina, I would be excluded from European aristocratic circles and the environment of royal families, no one spoke of it again because the Shah of Iran introduced us to all his guests of noble blood as newlyweds, "just married." Everyone was there, including my cousins; everyone congratulated us and gave us their best wishes. Witnesses at our church wedding were Jacques Piccard, my former tutor, Rober de Balkany, my sister Ella's husband, Corrado Agusta, Pahlavi, the son of the Shah's twin sister.

At that point, I returned to Geneva and hosted an event to celebrate our marriage, with a thousand guests, where my mother and my paternal aunt Maria (who was also my baptismal godmother) attended. Simeone of Bulgaria, my cousin, and many others were also present. My father only came later, for Emanuele Filiberto's baptism, of which he was the godfather.

Chapter 14

ROYAL CAREER

In the coastal village of La Panne, Belgium, about thirty kilometers west of Ostend and on the border with France, it was a very hot evening. Two young people walked arm in arm, exchanging affectionate gestures, taking advantage of the darkness. Suddenly, the man, dressed as a lieutenant, broke away from the embrace and stood at attention, giving a military salute.

"Your Majesty, I must confess that I am here with my wife," the young officer stammered nervously.

"I am here with mine too," Alberto I, King of the Belgians, replied with a smile, holding Queen Elisabeth's arm. This was the familiar and affectionate, yet ironic, interaction that my grandfather had with his subjects.

On August 4, 1914, Maria José turned eight years old. On that day, the Germans invaded Belgium. The country, created by European powers at the Conference of London in 1830 with the guarantee of "perpetual neutrality," saw its peace violated. This would happen again in the Second World War, except that the soldiers' helmets would bear a sinister swastika instead of a Prussian spike. My mother celebrated her birthday not with a cake and candles, but by going with her family to parliament to listen to her father, Albert I, King of the Belgians since 1909, urging the people to resist and unite against the German invader.

Shortly after, Maria José went into her first exile, in England, and then returned to La Panne, behind the lines of the final front against the Germans, behind the Yser River, where she shared the war's experiences with her active mother—bombings, hospitals, the tragedies of young lives lost. My grandmother, from the Bavarian Wittelsbach family, was of German culture but did not hesitate to support Belgium in both World Wars. My mother witnessed two invasions of her country and the devastation of Italy between the Nazis and Fascists, before embarking on her second exile at the age of forty with four children.

One day, a proud lady of noble lineage said to my mother, "Your Highness, my family is older than yours."

"That's true," Maria José replied with a smile, "but mine has had a more successful career."

This was my mother's character—someone who could move from the most ferocious irony to utter disdain for danger. In both cases, without hesitation or remorse afterward. A spontaneity that she would have appreciated— "Italian." My mother's family, the Wittelsbach dynasty, is probably older than even the Capetian dynasty, a lineage of dreamers and artists with great enthusiasm and great disappointments. Monaco di Baviera, which was a kingdom from 1806 to 1871, became a sort of German Florence under that dynasty. The famous Ludwig and his Walhalla, the legendary Empress Elisabeth (Sissi), my grandmother's aunt and wife of Emperor Franz Joseph of Austria-Hungary, and Maria, consort of the last King of the Two Sicilies, Francesco II. Additionally, the Saxe-Coburg and Gotha family of my mother's father. At the end of the 19th century, this dynasty sat on the thrones of half of Europe, firmly established. Thus, my mother grew up in Belgium, a young nation but already with universal suffrage, compulsory military service, and a socialist-style welfare system. Above all, from an early age, she knew that Belgium's governance depended solely on the favor of the people, who were already divided, at times fiercely, between Walloons and Flemish. Coming from a court where everyone knew how to do everything and was responsible for everything, she arrived in Italy—a country with a contrast between the formal and conservative etiquettes of the House of Savoy and the parvenu vulgarity of the Fascist hierarchs. In some post-war memoirs of certain German officers from the Prussian aristocracy—published long after the war—it was clearly written that both in Italy and Germany, the couple of Prince Umberto and Maria José was not well regarded by the Nazi and Fascist leaders. Hitler and Mussolini imposed parade-style grandiosity, as if made of cardboard, as Trilussa would say. However, my parents were brought up with absolute rigor, without privileges, without luxuries. Hitler himself no longer wanted my father in Germany after discovering that the German crowds were highly attracted to this handsome Italian prince, whose simple and polite manners highlighted the coarseness of Himmler, Goring, Goebbels, and even Hitler himself. Similarly, Mussolini couldn't stand the success of this young and beautiful royal couple, and he would have willingly replaced them with more obedient descendants of the Aosta branch.

One day, I was with my grandmother Elisabeth of Belgium and curiously observing a cabinet full of seemingly insignificant objects. My grandmother was a refined person with great humanistic culture, and I wondered why those objects held a place in her life, especially in a showcase outside her room. I was curious and asked her about it.

"Pick one of those objects and bring it to me, please," she said to me. I went and returned with a powder compact, which I chose because it was placed between two silver canaries that I had given to my grandmother, and from which she had never wanted to part.

"This is a gift someone gave me some years ago," she said, looking at the powder compact as if it were a relic, "a woman from the people, one of many citizens who come to me because they have problems." I asked her about the reason for that gift.

"It was a thank you for what I had done for her. It is an object of bad taste, but for me, it is worth more than a piece of jewelry." Reluctantly, Queen Elisabeth told me—because my mother never spoke about the good deeds she did for others—about a mother who had written to her that her son had returned from the Belgian Congo with a work-related injury. He had set up a stall to sell small items, but the municipal guards, instigated by local shopkeepers, fined him because he didn't have a proper permit.

The queen had gone to the stall in a village outside Brussels. She met the mother and her son, then went to the municipal bureaucrat who, even in the presence of the queen, resisted granting the sales license. The queen ordered him to give the license, which she then handed to the vendor. But the mother's heart was not at ease, and she told the queen that her invalid son would still be persecuted by the other shopkeepers. My grandmother was quick-witted—she took a sign and, in her own handwriting, wrote on it, "Supplier to the Royal Household." She smiled as she bought some merchandise and paid for it, giving meaning to the writing. Finally, the elderly woman insisted and gifted my grandmother the object she considered the most precious among the items for sale—the powder compact.

My mother, like my grandmother, greatly valued what is now called privacy. She found one of the few advantages of exile to be free from etiquettes and able to dress comfortably. One thing that particularly bothered her during her sixteen years in Italy was the presence of spies. Mussolini's notorious Ovra constantly monitored my parents day and night, controlling even Mussolini himself. My mother grew up with parents who, as reigning monarchs, rode motorcycles alone throughout Belgium without any security detail. Her father, Albert, spent days alone in the mountains on his climbing expeditions. On one occasion in Cortina, with a guide who was an ardent republican, he found himself incognito in a mountain hut. When they discovered who he was, he had already charmed everyone with his simplicity and, above all, with his physical endurance that few could match. My mother was also a formidable mountain walker, but now, looking back, I realize that her sports activities were also a way for her to assert her independence. What you achieve with your own legs does not depend on your surname, but only on your tenacity and inner strength.

With all this said, it doesn't mean that my mother didn't love Italy or the Italians; quite the opposite. She was attracted, as I still am today, by the spontaneity, the warmth, the languages and dialects, and the irony of a people that can demonstrate its humanity even in the most dramatic hours. She developed a deep affection for Naples, but she often told me that the most beautiful period of her life was the one spent at Poggio Imperiale (aside from the Joyeuse Entrée when, at twelve years old, she returned on horseback with her family to a Brussels liberated from the Germans) during the years from 1917 to 1919.

The Convent of the Santissima Annunziata, when it bears that name in Savoy history! It was founded in 1823 by Marianna Carolina of Saxony on Via della Scala in Florence. In 1860, it moved to the Villa Granducale degli Asburgo-Lorena at Poggio Imperiale, donated by Vittorio Emanuele II as a suitable location for a boarding school for noble girls. In one of the rooms, there is a plaque commemorating the fire in the cradle of the future first King of Italy. From the mists of the North, my mother and my grandmother arrived in Florence and began a frenetic tour of all the works of art in the city.

At Poggio Imperiale, you would arrive via a long avenue that ascended from Porta Romana, lined with a double row of cypress trees. Especially in the summer, it was the preferred residence of Maria Teresa of Austria-Lorraine with her son Vittorio Emanuele of Savoy. My mother studied there for two years, enlivening the college with her famous pranks and already displaying her leadership qualities. As it was trendy back then to have nicknames, my mother chose "Magi" for herself, short for Maria Giuseppina. That "José" came from the Portuguese branch of the Braganza family on her side, which had been Italianized to Giuseppina. Her great friend became Philipotte, the nickname for Bossilka Schaulich, Queen Elena's niece and, consequently, the great-granddaughter of Montenegro's Tsar Nicholas Petrovic Njegos. But my mother—another indicative anecdote of her character—constantly wrote to her parents in Belgium because she couldn't stand sitting at the table with the headmistress and teachers, separated from her classmates. To compensate for the isolation imposed by her status, my mother started using the informal "tu" with her fellow students at Poggio, scandalizing the English governess.

I remember once a delegation of Poggio Imperiale students came to visit Merlinge. My mother, who very rarely had strong emotions and even less so showed them, was truly moved that time and happy that a piece of her childhood returned to her after so many years.

My mother also said that her family, unlike the Savoyards, had the fortune of not being a hereditary one. Her father, Albert, became king in 1909 only because his uncle Leopold II's only male heir had died prematurely at the age of ten. Even though the Belgian crown was less strict behind closed doors, my father's family had an even freer lifestyle than was customary at that time. While my grandmother Elisabeth criticized her aunt, Empress Sissi, for her ostentatious behavior, she later scandalized the world herself when, already not so young, she traveled everywhere, including communist countries, to meet Mao, Castro, and Khrushchev. "Red Queen" they called my grandmother, and "Red Queen" they called my mother. In my opinion, they weren't so politically inclined; they simply loved traveling, getting to know new worlds, new people, and, above all, they truly did not care about other people's opinions and the rigid formal behavior of the royal household.

I discovered my mother late in life when we lived together in Merlinge, even though she always had her engagements, concerts, and meetings with artists and intellectuals. Sometimes, I managed to convince her to take a trip, or vice versa, she asked me to leave suddenly. One day, Maria José said to me, "Shall we go to Belgium together?"

I immediately replied, "No problem, I'll fill up the car, and we'll go."

I had a map of the roads, which were not like they are now, and there were no highways. The two of us went alone in my Ferrari. Before Reims, I stepped on the gas, going at 250 kilometers per hour. My mother commented, "At what speed are you going? 250 kilometers per hour? You know your uncle's car is faster?" She was talking about my uncle Leopold's Ferrari, who was the King of Belgium and also had a Bugatti. Then, in Reims, we stopped at a champagne producer's facility, where we were invited for breakfast and a visit. It was a wonderful trip with my mother, but we had other enjoyable journeys. The longest we took was from Geneva to Lisbon by car. At the time, my mother had a six-cylinder Fiat with right-hand drive and a special body, and I had to sit in the front; otherwise, I'd get sick. Behind us were my mother and madame C. On the second trip, also from Geneva to Lisbon, I traveled with monsieur C., but in a Topolino, the small Fiat; it was like going there by... bicycle!

Undoubtedly, among the many journeys she took, the most emotional for my mother was her return to Italy. Lawyer D'Amelio, who had been the legal representative of my grandfather, my father, and myself—a wonderful person—worked to obtain an Italian passport for my mother after my father's passing. When the passport was ready, Maria José returned to Italy on March 1, 1988, accompanied by my sister Maria Gabriella, and she began her tour starting from the Aosta Valley.

Much has been said about the type of relationship between my father and my mother, especially in recent times. The fact remains that my mother chose room 609 when she was admitted to the Geneva Canton Hospital. It was in that room that my father Umberto passed away at seventy-nine years old on March 18, 1983, and in that same room, my mother Maria José passed away at ninety-four years old on January 27, 2001.

My mother was in love with Naples and Posillipo, where we spent the happiest moments of our childhood. However, for reasons I cannot quite pinpoint, she also mentioned Tuscany and Poggio Imperiale, where she had lived from eleven to thirteen years old, as the happiest time of her life. The most witty and succinct description of her personality comes from the pen of a Tuscan, Indro Montanelli: "Precisely because she was not very Italian, she would have made a magnificent queen: without the boorish exhibitionism of our republican first ladies, but with a strict sense of duty and manners, whose simplicity only served to emphasize her royalty."

Chapter 15

DAMNED COURTIERS

It is likely that if my grandfather, Victor Emmanuel III, had not accepted coexistence with fascism, at least not under the conditions that caused so much suffering to the Italian people and our family, the monarchy would not have collapsed.

Of course, I too would have wanted to save the crown in all circumstances, but I am convinced that the only viable path would have been to abdicate: King Victor Emmanuel III abdicates in favor of his son, Umberto II, and potentially remains as an advisor but out of the spotlight. I would have done it as a surprise, from one day to the next, informing only the highest military leaders and no one else. The military was with the Savoia, not with Mussolini, and they would have been ready to maintain public order in case of any reactions from the fascist bosses.

It would have been a peaceful coup, without arrests and bloodshed. Thus, neither my grandfather, having just relinquished the crown, nor my father, just seated as king, would have had to sign the laws imposed by Mussolini anymore. An abrupt abdication would have been a surprise to everyone, a bloodless coup. But it should have been done much earlier than July 1943 when Mussolini fell, and the Allies landed in Sicily.

The people were long tired of war and fascism, and by preparing a secret agreement with the Allies, they would have ensured that the Allies occupied Italy before the Germans. Only after the fall of Mussolini on July 25, 1943, did Hitler, even more furious than before, send his divisions to occupy Italy and began plotting, among other things, the kidnapping of the Savoia family. In reality, to further distance Casa Savoia from Mussolini, the masterpiece of the double abdication should have been achieved: King Victor Emmanuel III abdicates in favor of his son Umberto II, who in turn abdicates - at the same time - in favor of his son Vittorio Emanuele, that is, in favor of me. However, since I was still a child - six years old in 1943 - I would have become the heir to the throne under the temporary regency of my mother, Maria José.

As I have already mentioned, this idea had already been proposed at the time by the philosopher Benedetto Croce, who was aware that my mother would have been able to negotiate with the Anglo-Americans and the Vatican for Italy's exit from the war and fascism. Let us not forget that the royal house of Belgium, my mother's family, was already known for its open, democratic ideas, tinged with socialism.

I believe, however, that unfortunately, my grandfather Victor Emmanuel III trusted only himself and did not consider his son Umberto mature and prepared enough to be king. Forgetting that my father was ignorant of government and crown matters precisely because he was not informed, in keeping with the Savoy motto "One reigns and commands one at a time." My grandfather was too centralized, deciding everything on his own, seldom listening to anyone's advice, much less his son Umberto's. I repeat, if he had abdicated in time, he might have been able to save Italy and the monarchy. Assuming, of course, that my grandfather the king could have accepted the hypothesis of the double abdication, many figures around him would have done everything to prevent it from happening for sure. Starting with Badoglio, who, indeed, became prime minister after Mussolini's fall and took hold of all power, abusing it quite a bit. Someone has written that Badoglio would have wanted to act as regent in place of my mother, Maria José, in the case of the double abdication. I am convinced he would have done so if it had suited him. Let's remember that Pietro Badoglio, from the defeat of Caporetto to the African campaign, from September 8 until the republic, always remained afloat with any government, maintaining good relations with Mussolini, the king, the Germans, the Allies, up to De Gasperi and Togliatti.

But there was no abdication, neither single nor double, and for us, the sad path of exile opened. When we were already living in Portugal, we received Belgian passports, but my father never wanted to use one. He always preferred to have the passport of the Order of Malta, which the Savoia consider their right. In our Portuguese exile, there was no way to engage in any political activity: we continued our lessons, and my father received various visitors.

Exile was particularly complicated for my mother, Maria José, who loved Italy and especially Naples very much. She was a passionate and enthusiastic traveler, and the most beautiful moments of our childhood were spent in Posillipo. However, she often spoke fondly of Tuscany and Poggio Imperiale, where she lived from the age of eleven to thirteen. These were the happiest moments of her life. And it was precisely from the pen of a Tuscan, Indro Montanelli, that the most acute and concise description of her character came: "Precisely because she was not very Italian, she would have made a magnificent queen: without the showy exhibitionism of our republican first ladies but with a strict sense of duty and manners that only served to underscore her royalty."

In the beginning, Umberto had daily contacts with Italy. Many had promised to keep him informed every day, and their relationship with him would be constant. However, gradually, these relationships became strained and less frequent. Within the family, the question of exile was never discussed or addressed in any way. Whenever I had doubts about what to do, I thought, "I trust my father, and I will follow his lead."

In Switzerland, I grew older and started to interact with various Italians who came to visit my father. Many of them idolized him, considering him a mythical figure, and openly expressed their affection for the monarchy and a king who had never abdicated.

Around the age of sixteen, things seemed to change. Groups of monarchists came to Merlinge to meet me, and discussions about Vittorio Emanuele started to circulate. But in reality, a significant portion of the figures surrounding my father took advantage of my inexperience and began to obstruct me, keeping me on the sidelines, subtly preventing any opportunity for us to discuss the monarchy, especially in detail. For them, creating a void around my father meant better manipulation. And indeed, they succeeded, driving us further apart. To illustrate how they managed to spoil our relationship, I can mention an incident: Umberto was about to leave for Montpellier, where his mother, Queen Elena, who passed away at the age of seventy-nine on November 28, 1952 (five years prior, on December 28, 1947, her husband, Vittorio Emanuele III, had died in Egypt at the age of seventy-eight). I asked him if I could accompany him, but he replied, "No, there's no need for you to go whimpering at your grandmother's grave when you've already caused enough trouble." Due to this painful misunderstanding, I retreated into myself even more and abandoned any further attempts to reconcile.

It was precisely at that time that a blessed day brought Franco Mattavelli into my life, a character who played a significant role in my life. My father sent him to me when I was already attending the University of Geneva, to support and guide me. Mattavelli was a former military man and monarchist, not part of my father's court, and from the start, he sought to shield me from the relentless accusations thrown at me by the courtiers. They claimed I had no interest in history, monarchy, or anything, for that matter. In reality, I tried to follow some things, but I always encountered a barrier, and no one helped me understand how I could enter the world of monarchists on my own at such a young age. That's when Mattavelli began taking me around, introducing me as the heir to the Savoia family. He introduced me to different people and organized various monarchist events. Meanwhile, he had to be cautious around the people who hovered around the court, but he got along well with Montezemolo, who, being a Navy officer accustomed to giving orders, could stand up to the courtiers and keep them in line.

With Mattavelli's arrival, I realized that I had an opportunity at hand to finally organize a monarchist group capable of countering the courtiers who besieged my father. This new group, led by Franco Mattavelli, would highlight the name of the Crown Prince in demonstrations and ceremonies. Finally, I would have the chance to address the public as a representative of the monarchists.

By now, I was becoming acquainted with the reality of associations and various monarchist groups. However, it seemed that their representatives were often more interested in discussing their party than the idea of monarchy itself or the need to create a movement of opinion. Several small groups continued to emerge, some less legitimately, aiming to support the monarchy, but in reality, they lacked a clear purpose and direction. Many of these movements were influenced and funded by Falcone Lucifero, a former minister of the Royal Household, and they would hold mostly ineffective speeches and conferences. These movements always sought their own interests without caring about the monarchy or the Savoia family. Certainly, if my father had returned, all of them would have disappeared or at least ceased hostilities towards me. It's essential to note that in Italy, the monarchists had previously enjoyed considerable support, but as always, internal conflicts ruined their popular appeal, and there were far too many internal and external disputes in the parliament.

During that period, the two leaders of the monarchist party, Lizzadri and Covelli, were too absorbed in their mutual competition and ambitions, which led to the destruction of a movement that had significant support in Italy, even within the parliament. As a result, the popular image of the monarchy faded away.

One day, I realized that I, too, should do something. I started writing for newspapers and expressing my views, also with the assistance of Mattavelli. I believed that I needed to make gestures that showed the monarchy's continued existence and provided a significant response to the many loyal supporters of my father. I particularly began speaking out about the anachronism of Article XIII of the Constitution, which prevented our return to Italy. One of the first Italian politicians who had claimed to address the issue of the Savoia family's exile was Craxi, but between words and deeds... nothing happened. Other Italian prime ministers had made favorable statements, but they remained just words without follow-through. Meanwhile, the courtiers continued their hostility, speaking ill of me and my real or alleged reckless actions to my father.

One painful incident occurred when I attended the memorial service for Queen Elena in Montpellier. I reported the event to my father in London, and he asked me to provide a written report on it. I handed over the two-page report, along with some photos of the service, to Coppola, an aide-de-camp of Umberto, with the intention that he would deliver it. However, I later learned that nothing had been delivered to my father, and my report with the photos was probably destroyed. This episode was just one of many examples of the war waged against me by my father's court, which intensified as he grew ill, and I became more aware of their deceptions.

I have previously mentioned how they tried to obstruct my relationship with Marina. Even though the dossier proving the nobility of my future wife's family had been sent and never reached my father's hands, he genuinely appreciated and valued Marina when he met her. Before that, Marina had already passed the test of my grandmother Elisabetta, the Queen of Belgium, who had invited and hosted her in her residence near the Royal Palace in Belgium for a month.

While my father was alive, I knew I couldn't take initiatives on my own. He would remind me that he needed to handle things, invoking the Savoia family motto, "I command one at a time."

After my father's passing, I realized that there were possibilities to bring the issue of my return to Italy before the European Parliament and the European Court of Human Rights in Strasbourg. Italy was in an atypical position within the European Union because it requested an exception to the free movement of people and goods, specifically concerning the return of the Savoia family to Italy. It was strange that Italy maintained the Savoia family's exile despite being outside the logic of European integration. The exile of the Savoia family remained in effect, even after the Schengen Agreement, which abolished many of the internal borders in Europe.

Filing a case against my own country at the European Court of Human Rights saddened me, and I never wanted to do so. However, I felt compelled to claim this elementary right. I want to respect the law, even if I find it absurd. That's why I am committed to abolishing this anachronistic law and have finally had my case accepted, with the recognition that exile is a violation of freedom.

I have never wanted to be involved in politics, although many times I have been asked to lead movements or political parties. Especially after my father's death, I became even more convinced that a monarchist party is not justified. If there is a king, there should not be a party because a king is "super partes" and represents the people, not a political party. I always agreed with my father when he said, "The monarchy will never be a party!"

When Umberto left Italy, some wanted to form a monarchist party, but I believe it was a big mistake. Instead of a party, they should have created a large movement by uniting all the existing monarchist associations in Italy under a federation, respecting their individual identities, to preserve the tradition of monarchy in Italy. However, the idea of a federation seemed difficult to apply, as even when I proposed it, they fought among themselves because each group wanted to be more important than the others or disagreed on the name, and so on. The goal of such an organization would have been to bring together all possible and imaginable monarchist ideas while maintaining the autonomy of each association to keep the monarchy's tradition alive in Italy without necessarily aiming for a return to power for the Savoia family.

Today, I see no need to restore a monarchy in Italy. We have nothing to support such a move, and it would be poorly executed without the support of a cohesive federation of all the existing monarchist realities. In Italy, a Latin country, an image representing national identity is required, as seen in Spain, for example, a neighboring country with similar characteristics. A king represents a nation, and in Europe, there are ten monarchies that function as national symbols. When the king reigns but does not govern, the monarchy can coexist very well with democratic institutions like the government and parliament. The monarch represents the nation and is a figure to whom any citizen can turn.

Unfortunately, many people fail to understand this. A true monarch is a charismatic figure but is also entirely at the disposal of their people. We all know that Italy cannot return to being a monarchy. I reiterate that I have never supported the idea of having a monarchist party. Unfortunately, I have dealt with individuals who insisted on pursuing their mistaken path, creating significant difficulties for me and consistently opposing me, even accusing me of being anti-monarchist. I am not anti-monarchist; I only support the existence of a monarchy in a country where the appropriate institutional conditions are present.

At the moment, I agree that Italy is fine as it is and doesn't need a monarchy. What it needs instead is a flag and symbols that confirm its national identity. For me, the monarchic spirit is rooted in the value of the homeland, understood in a modern and current sense. However, I reiterate that this does not imply seeking to have a king or queen for Italy. Today, it is challenging to recreate a sense of unity and national identity as it perhaps was during the time of fighting for the country's liberation from foreign powers. Therefore, it would make sense to reintroduce the Savoy shield in the flag, as that symbol is part of Italy's history.

People enjoy the idea of monarchy beyond its political power, and this shared sentiment could strengthen national identity. The monarchy should remain above the political parties, representing unity and support for the democratic republic. Regardless of people's political affiliations - whether left, center, or right - the monarchy serves as a unifying symbol. It is crucial to respect the flag, and I hope to never read in the newspapers about the tricolor being burned or considered as worthless... or worse.

In Europe, there are examples of constitutional monarchies that coexist harmoniously with modernity. In some cases, the monarchy has been the only institution keeping a country together, like in Belgium, where Flemish and Walloon communities coexist. Another significant example is Bulgaria, where my cousin Simeone, son of my aunt Giovanna di Savoia, would be the king but prefers to remain prime minister. In his role as prime minister, he believes he can better assist his country than as a king or president.

What's essential to me is to return to my homeland and work for my country. Even when abroad, I have always worked for Italian companies, contributing to my country's interests. I have offered my services all around the world and, if given the opportunity, I could be of assistance to small and medium-sized Italian businesses, introducing them to international markets, with the support of the state. Such a strategy, similar to what our French competitors have always implemented, could be beneficial for Italy.

Throughout these long and seemingly endless years of exile, what has always supported and comforted me is the affection of Italians, both those in Italy and those abroad. I have always classified Italians into three groups: the first group includes my family, relatives, and Casa Savoia; the second group consists of politicians; and the third group, the Italian people. I love the true Italians, as they are simple and kind-hearted. I have worked with and for them all over the world. From those Italians, I have received touching letters that have moved me to tears, filled with kindness and genuine sentiment. To the best of my abilities, I have always replied to them, by hand, of course. I remember receiving a letter from an entire school after my father's death, with exceptional and heartfelt words.

Additionally, I have accumulated countless postcards from Italy, with just "Vittorio Emanuele, Geneva" as the address, and they still reach me. I should write to the Swiss Post to thank them. I have amassed dozens of albums of Italian postcards, possibly the most extensive collection in the world, even with some addressed to my son, Emanuele Filiberto. These postcards have allowed me, indirectly, to "see" Italy, including its less known and hidden aspects.

When I meet Italian tourists who recognize me, they overwhelm me with warm greetings and questions like, "Why don't you join us? We'll take you back to Italy, no problem." Then we take pictures together, and someone from the group usually goes to the bus and brings me something, a bottle of wine, a cheese wheel, and gifts it to me, saying that they are honored if I accept a product from their land. I experience these encounters as a form of compensation for the injustice of being kept away from my homeland. I have never encountered any criticism or negative remarks from the Italians I have met; perhaps they lacked the courage, but every time, I feel their genuine affection and support.

Believe it or not, from the Italian people, even during my exile, I have always received kindness and affection. Always. One episode that stands out in my memory with great pleasure is when I was working with Corrado Agusta, dealing with helicopters, and attending the two important aerospace exhibitions in Europe: Farnborough in England and Le Bourget in France.

At the old Le Bourget airport in Paris, where the fair takes place, we were waiting for an American transport aircraft belonging to the Italian Air Force. When it arrived, the crew joined us for lunch, and Corrado Agusta kindly introduced me to the commander. The conversation was enjoyable, and my passion for flying becomes evident when talking about planes.

After lunch, the commander invited me to visit his aircraft, and naturally, I accepted enthusiastically. To my delight, I found a heartwarming surprise on board. The commander had the pilots and flight crew - about six or seven people - change into their uniforms, and he himself wore his uniform. They all saluted me and then took me to the cockpit, where, together with the commander, I guided the plane to the parking area. But it didn't end there: after this small ceremony, the commander also gifted me his decorations. Such experiences are truly unforgettable. It's worth noting that, as a young boy, my dream was to become a pilot in the air force. However, since I couldn't serve in the Italian military, I had considered enlisting in the Belgian Air Force. My father opposed this idea, fearing a possible war between Italy and Belgium.

Throughout my life, I have encountered disillusionment with the political aspects of Italy, but on the other hand, the Italian people and their demonstrations of affection have always supported me, providing the deepest and most meaningful comfort during my fifty-six years of exile.

I have noticed an interesting phenomenon; among the thousands of displays of support and affection I have received from Italians, most of them come from young people. One might assume that young individuals would know less about history compared to their elders, who lived through significant events. However, many young Italians have been present in my life, especially during moments of mourning, such as the funerals of my father in 1983 and my mother in 2001. It still surprises me when young people I meet in public, whether alone, in groups, or as couples, approach me, greet me, and ask for a photograph together or an autograph. To them, and to all Italians who show their affection, I say thank you.

In Italy, monarchy no longer has a reason to exist. My father had come to this conviction in his later years, although he was deeply attached to preserving the chivalric orders of the Savoia family. In our millennial tradition, like other European dynasties, we established and managed the so-called chivalric orders. Historically, knights were aristocrats who defended Christianity and, consequently, protected the weak and oppressed. Over time, this privilege extended to individuals of high moral standing who earned knighthood on the battlefield, with the traditional accolade of the sword on the shoulder. The primary purpose of the sword was defense rather than offense.

The chivalric orders of the House of Savoia are three: the Order of the Annunziata, the Order of Saints Maurice and Lazarus (also known as the Mauriziano), and the Order of Merit, which replaced the Order of the Crown of Italy (now abolished). When my father passed away, I found a very ancient stone in one of his drawers, which belonged to the ring of the Order of Mauriziano.

The stone had been lost since before the French Revolution and was reestablished by Charles Albert. Tradition dictated that the symbol of the order was a ring with an oval agate stone, engraved with a knight, which once belonged to Saint Maurice. This led me to consider the revival of the chivalric order of Saints Maurice and Lazarus, and I began to study the relevant documents and issues.

Saint Maurice was a Roman centurion of African origin, commanding the Theban Legion composed of 6,666 Egyptian soldiers, all Christians. This legion was sent from North Africa to Gaul (present-day France) in the third century AD. According to legend, Maurice and some of his soldiers were martyred by the pagan Emperor Maximian in Valais, Switzerland. The current town of Sankt Moritz in Switzerland, known in German as San Maurizio, is named after him. The events surrounding the Roman centurion immediately sparked widespread popular devotion, which was organized and established as the Order of Saints Maurice and Lazarus by Amedeo VI of Savoia, also known as the Green Count, who had also introduced the blue scarf for officers, still worn by military and national Italian sports teams today. When the House of Savoia took possession of the territories in the Valle d'Aosta, they also inherited the veneration of the Order. Over time, the Order regained strength and importance, enduring through the era of the Crusades and beyond, along with other significant chivalric orders such as the Order of Saint Lazarus, the Order of the Knights of Saint John (later becoming the Order of Malta), the Teutonic Knights, and more.

Amedeo VIII, who was elected Pope as Felix V at the Council of Basel in 1439, then abdicated ten years later to resolve the Papal schism, founded the first monastery of Saint Maurice in Ripaille on Lake Geneva. Later, Emanuele Filiberto, known as "Iron Head," revitalized the Order of Mauriziano, which was officially recognized by Pope Gregory XIII in 1572. Gregory XIII designated Emanuele Filiberto and his successors as Grand Masters of the Order. With a subsequent papal bull, the Orders of Saints Maurice and Lazarus were unified.

When I resumed the activities of the Order of Mauriziano, we had fewer than fifteen knights; now we have approximately three thousand. The Order functions well; we have a council, a treasurer, and we carry out significant charitable projects, focusing on providing equipment rather than monetary donations. For example, we donated equipment to the Gaslini Hospital in Genoa and made other important interventions in Albania,

Bulgaria, and Argentina. In the future, we plan to establish a boarding school for children in Naples.

Presently, I am dedicated to the activities of the Orders, although it can be challenging to manage members when the council convenes. Often, they argue, each one insisting on being right. My son is the Grand Chancellor, and he couldn't believe what he witnessed during some meetings. Once, I was almost tempted to propose, as is done in church during Mass, that everyone exchange a sign of peace. Nonetheless, participating in council meetings with my son is a pleasant duty because we understand each other well. Emanuele Filiberto speaks first, then I follow, and finally, we address the agenda items. The annual membership fee is quite low, contrary to what some

might believe, even lower than that of the Order of Malta. We have a fund, receive donations and legacies, and twice a year, we organize a charity gala. Guests, in addition to the entrance ticket, are encouraged to buy lottery tickets and participate in the auction. Each illustrious attendee donates something for the auction, either items or services. Last year, I offered a long weekend at my home in Cavallo. As for the lottery, luxury shops provide the prizes, while individual attendees offer items for the auction. Every year, we hold the Chapter ceremony, during which new knights are appointed, followed by a dance, lottery, and charity auction.

As the Grand Master of the Order of Mauriziano, I am by right also a member of the Order of Malta, whose Grand Bailiff is Collar of the Annunziata. My father conferred upon me the Grand Collar of the Annunziata on September 18, 1964, in Athens, during the wedding of King Constantine of Greece to Princess Anne-Marie of Denmark. Constantine had recently ascended to the throne of Greece following the death of his father, King Paul, the husband of Queen Frederica, who had organized the cruise on the Agamemnon, leading to royal marriages.

This Grand Collar of the Annunziata was quite delicate, and one link had broken. People immediately informed my father that Vittorio had broken the Collar. He responded with kindness, saying, "Next time, during the next ceremony, you and I will wear the Grand Collar of the Annunziata together." Unfortunately, there was no opportunity to wear it together again.

The other Collar of the Annunziata belonged to Cardinal Casaroli, the Secretary of State of the Vatican, and one should be given to Monsignor Sodano, the current Secretary of State, who expressed a desire for me to personally present it to him in the Vatican.

The organization of the Order of Mauriziano consists of delegates from various countries and regions of Italy. We do not cover the entire world, but we have created a solid network that continues to grow. Each delegate is responsible for organizing a lunch twice a year, where all knights in their area of jurisdiction gather to discuss and plan. In addition to delegates in Europe, we have a delegate in the United States, New York, who works exceptionally well with overwhelming enthusiasm, another in Brazil, one in Argentina - where things are progressing slowly due to the country's difficult situation - and one soon to be established in Japan, as well as a female delegate in Monte Carlo. In short, the Order has awakened from its slumber and is in excellent health. We have had medals minted, and each member possesses the red mantle of the Order, while the ladies have a beautiful black cape with the cross of Saint Maurice on the shoulder.

To some, it may seem anachronistic to preserve ancient traditions and continue wearing Knight's mantles. However, as I have often stated, a millennia-old dynasty is not just part of history; it is history. Let these symbols survive, allowing young people to learn about the ideals and styles of monarchy.

The End

BIOGRAPHY

Alexandra Sterling is a dedicated historian with a profound passion for Italian history. Born and raised in the heart of Alabama, she found herself captivated by the rich cultural heritage of Italy from a young age. Her insatiable curiosity and love for historical narratives led her on a remarkable journey of exploration into the annals of Italian royalty, particularly the exile of Vittorio Emanuele III, the former King of Italy.

Drawing inspiration from her academic background in history and her genuine fascination with Italian culture, Alexandra embarked on a scholarly quest to uncover the intricacies of Vittorio Emanuele III's exile. With meticulous research and unwavering ardor, she delved into archives, historical documents, and personal accounts to paint a vivid and compelling picture of this lesser-known chapter in Italian history.

As a historian, Alexandra Sterling is renowned for her keen eye for detail and her ability to breathe life into forgotten stories. Her works resonate with readers worldwide, as she expertly weaves together historical facts and human emotions, transporting them to a bygone era.

When she's not immersed in her historical research, Alexandra enjoys immersing herself in Italian literature and cuisine, indulging in the sights and sounds of Italy during her frequent visits. Her love for the country and its history continues to inspire her work, leaving an indelible mark on the hearts of her readers and the world of historical research alike.

LIFE OF
STARS

9 798223 090502